D1488032

To: Best
      with love
From:
      Sue

First Aid
for the
HEART

Compiled by Beth Mende Conny

Illustrated by Steve Haskamp

PETER PAUPER PRESS, INC.
WHITE PLAINS, NEW YORK

For Joe, always

Illustrations copyright © 2001
Steve Haskamp

Designed by Heather Zschock

Text copyright © 2001
Peter Pauper Press, Inc.
202 Mamaroneck Avenue
White Plains, NY 10601
ISBN 0-88088-549-1
Printed in China
7 6 5 4 3 2

Visit us at www.peterpaper.com

First Aid
for the
HEART

INTRODUCTION

LOVE. It's such a simple word, and yet it captures so much.

TO BE IN LOVE is to explore the depths of another's heart, while learning more about one's own. **TO BE IN LOVE** is to be in life— fully, madly, deeply—and to grow with each experience.

Sometimes, this growth comes easily; other times it's a challenge. Love, after all, has so many shades, not to mention ups and downs. Each fluctuation,

however, gives us a fuller
understanding of love's complex
nature.

Let *First Aid for the Heart* help
deepen that understanding.
Within its pages, you'll find
words to capture the many forms
and meanings of love. Taken
together, these inspiring words
provide new ways to celebrate
love: the simplest and most
profound of all emotions.

B. M. C.

Love
is
a
verb.

EILEEN FLANAGAN

WE LOVE because
it is the only
true adventure.

NIKKI GIOVANNI

In our life there
is a single color, as on
an artist's palette,
which provides the
meaning of life and art.
It is the color of love.

MARC CHAGALL

When two people
LOVE EACH OTHER,
they don't look
at each other,
they look in the
same direction.

GINGER ROGERS

Everyone makes mistakes. To forgive those mistakes is the **ACTION OF LOVE.** To forgive strengthens our love.

JOHN GRAY

No one dies of
a broken heart.
Put together and given
a reasonable rest cure,
an old ticker will get
into almost as much
fascinating trouble as
a brand new one.

LOUISE BAKER

Love doesn't make
the world go 'round.
Love is what makes
the ride worthwhile.

FRANKLIN P. JONES

You will find as you look
back upon your life that the
moments when you have
really lived are the moments
when you have done things
in the **SPIRIT OF LOVE.**

HENRY DRUMMOND

The tender words
we said to one another
are stored in the secret
heart of heaven:
One day like rain they
will fall and spread,
and our mystery will grow
green over the world.

RUMI

I don't want
to live—
I want to
love first,
and live
incidentally.

ZELDA FITZGERALD

To be a lover
is not to
make love,
but to find
a new way
to live.

PAUL LA COUR

[L]ove is like a precious plant. You can't just accept it and leave it in the cupboard or just think it's going to get on by itself. You've got to keep watering it.

JOHN LENNON

We attract hearts
by the qualities we
display: we retain
them by the qualities
we possess.

JEAN BAPTISTE
ANTOINE SUARD

It is only with
the heart that one
can see rightly;
what is essential is
invisible to the eye.

**ANTOINE
DE SAINT-EXUPÉRY**

GREAT LOVE

can both
take hold
and let go.

R. ORAGE

To keep the fire burning
brightly there's one easy rule:
Keep the two logs together,
near enough to keep each
other warm and far enough
apart—about a finger's
breadth—for breathing room.

MARNIE REED CROWELL

Love is what
you've been
through with
somebody.

JAMES THURBER

You can give
without loving
but you can't
love without
giving.

AMY CARMICHAEL

Love rules without rules.

ITALIAN PROVERB

Relationships are assignments.
They are part of a vast plan
for our enlightenment,
the Holy Spirit's blueprint
by which each individual
soul is led to greater
awareness and expanded love.

MARIANNE WILLIAMSON

Love is a fruit in
season at all times,
and within reach
of every hand.

MOTHER TERESA

If your head tells you
one thing and your heart
tells you another,
before you do anything,
you should first decide
whether you have a better
head or a better heart.

MARILYN VOS SAVANT

LOVE IS ALWAYS OPEN ARMS. If you close your arms about love you will find that you are left holding only yourself.

LEO BUSCAGLIA

Let there be spaces
in your togetherness
and let the winds of
the heavens dance
between you.

KAHLIL GIBRAN

Love is generally confused with dependence; but in point of fact, you can love only in proportion to your capacity for independence.

ROLLO MAY

[S]piritual partners are
able to see clearly that there
is indeed a deeper reason why
they are together, and that
that reason has a great deal
to do with the evolution
of their souls.

GARY ZUKAV

Our daily existence requires
both closeness and distance,
the wholeness of self, the
wholeness of intimacy.
We reconcile oneness and
separateness through ordinary
earthbound human love.

JUDITH VIORST

Among those whom
I like or admire, I can find
no common denominator,
but among those whom
I love, I can: all of them
make me laugh.

W. H. AUDEN

Relationships
are mirrors
of ourselves.

LOUISE L. HAY

Do not rely on gestures
or outer appearances
as an indication of the love
that people have for you.
Rely instead on the
feeling of love
that exists between you.

SANAYA ROMAN

The meeting of two
personalities is like
the contact of two
chemical substances:
if there is any reaction,
both are transformed.

CARL JUNG

Love is being stupid together.

PAUL VALÉRY

[F]or one human being
to love another:
that is perhaps the most
difficult task of all . . . ,
the work for which all other
work is but preparation.

RAINER MARIA RILKE

Only through our
CONNECTEDNESS
to others can we really
know and enhance the
self. And only through
working on the self can
we begin to enhance
our connectedness
to others.

HARRIET GOLDHOR LERNER

It's not easy to generalize about love. Like each person who feels its invisible filaments stretching to another person, it is unique in each instance.

GLORIA STEINEM

There is no
surprise more magical
than the surprise
of being loved;
it is God's finger
on man's shoulder.

 CHARLES MORGAN

There is no
remedy for love
but to love more.

HENRY DAVID THOREAU

Love is but the
discovery of ourselves
in others, and the
delight in the
recognition.

ALEXANDER SMITH

I relax my rigid ideas about what love should look like. I open to love's infinite variety.

JULIA CAMERON

Love has nothing to
do with what you are
expecting to get—
only with what you are
expecting to give—
which is everything.

KATHARINE HEPBURN

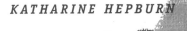

I think the reason people seek romance is that they want to step into the field of infinite possibilities with someone. They want to share the experience of another world in which two people share the unknown together.

DEEPAK CHOPRA

There are no boundaries when we fully embrace each other.

THOMAS CRUM

**Understanding moods
is as important to
people in relationships
as understanding
weather is to
an airplane pilot.**

*RICHARD CARLSON AND
JOSEPH BAILEY*

That is the true season of love, when we believe that we alone can love, that no one could ever have loved so before us, and that no one will love in the same way after us.

GOETHE

Love understands love; it needs no talk.

F. R. HAVERGAL

Those who live
passionately teach
us how to love.
Those who love
passionately teach
us how to live.

*SARAH BAN
BREATHNACH*

Acknowledge and
respect your differences.
You and your partner
are not identical twins.

RIKI ROBBINS JONES

Our choice of partners
is perhaps the clearest
single statement of our
choice of values.

WARREN FARRELL

Choose love because we've
known it was the right choice
ever since we bit the apple.
We are on our path, love is our
purpose, and that stretch is our
next step forward. If not you,
then who? If not now, then
when? **CHOOSE LOVE.**

JUDITH SILLS

Redeemed and restored,
love returns us to the
promise of everlasting life.
When we love we can
let our hearts speak.

BELL HOOKS

Love doesn't sit
there like a stone,
it has to be made,
like bread;
remade all the time,
made new.

URSULA K. LE GUIN

[A relationship is] about two people having tremendous weaknesses and vulnerabilities, like we all do, and one person being able to strengthen the other in their areas of vulnerability. And vice versa. **YOU NEED EACH OTHER.** You bolster each other.

JANE FONDA

It was worth every minute.
The happiness and the pain
were like exercises for my heart,
each time leaving it in better
shape than before.

KIMBERLY KIRBERGER

**[LOVE] REALLY *IS*
WORTH FIGHTING FOR,**
being brave for,
risking everything for.
And the trouble is,
if you don't risk anything,
you risk even *more*.

ERICA JONG

Commitment is
the keystone of
a relationship,
the wedge-shaped
stone of an arch
that locks its parts
together in love.

ALEXANDRA STODDARD

The heart is a living museum.
In each of its galleries,
no matter how narrow or
dimly lit, preserved forever
like wondrous diatoms,
are our moments of loving
and being loved.

DIANE ACKERMAN

If you can learn
from hard knocks,
you can also learn
from soft touches.

CAROLYN KENMORE

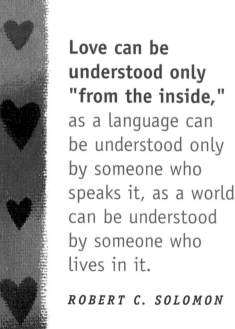

Love can be understood only "from the inside," as a language can be understood only by someone who speaks it, as a world can be understood by someone who lives in it.

ROBERT C. SOLOMON

If you *think* there is only one true love and you've found it—maybe even years *after* high school—fine. Many of us don't belong to the once-in-a-lifetime crowd. We think you're missing *a lot*.

HELEN GURLEY BROWN

The story of a love is not important—what is important is that one is capable of love. It is perhaps the only glimpse we are permitted of eternity.

HELEN HAYES

[A] true soul mate is
a soul bound to yours by
a profound and timeless
level of **love, trust,
and devotion . . .**

BARBARA DE ANGELIS

A wise heart flourishes not tentatively but with all the determination and courage of a woman who has decided that her pain will not turn to bitterness and that loss can be a begin-ning, not an end. It chooses to risk loving because its natural impulse is to open, not close.

SUSAN FORWARD

YOU DON'T HAVE TO DO ANYTHING TO FIND LOVE. Love will come into your life if you simply remove the obstacles that are standing in its way. And we start the process by creating love not tomorrow but today, *right now*.

LAURA DAY

Falling in love and staying in
love requires its own kind of
heroism. If we are to experience
intimacy, our hearts have to be
brave as well as loving. That's
because it takes real courage to
love; it takes real courage to
make a commitment.

STEVEN CARTER

The loving are
the daring.

BAYARD TAYLOR